TINA FEY

KATHRYN HARRISON

THE
GIANTS
OF COMEDY™

TINA FEY

KATHRYN HARRISON

ROSEN
PUBLISHING®

New York

Published in 2016 by The Rosen Publishing Group, Inc.
29 East 21st Street, New York, NY 10010

Copyright © 2016 by The Rosen Publishing Group, Inc.

First Edition

Library of Congress Cataloging-in-Publication Data

Names: Harrison, Kathryn, 1987-
Title: Tina Fey / Kathryn Harrison.
Description: First edition. | New York : Rosen Publishing, 2016. | Series:
  The giants of comedy | Includes bibliographical references and index.
Identifiers: LCCN 2015036536 | ISBN 9781499462562 (library bound)
Subjects: LCSH: Fey, Tina, 1970—Juvenile literature. | Television actors
  and actresses—United States—Biography—Juvenile literature. | Women
  television writers—United States—Biography—Juvenile literature. | Women
  comedians—United States—Biography—Juvenile literature.
Classification: LCC PN2287.F4255 H37 2016 | DDC 791.4502/8092—dc23
LC record available at http://lccn.loc.gov/2015036536

Manufactured in the United States of America

CONTENTS

6 INTRODUCTION

10 CHAPTER ONE Back to the Roots

24 CHAPTER TWO Finding Herself

43 CHAPTER THREE *Saturday Night Live*

56 CHAPTER FOUR *30 Rock*

68 CHAPTER FIVE Fey and Film

78 CHAPTER SIX The Next Chapter for Tina Fey

92 Fact Sheet on Tina Fey
93 Fact Sheet on Tina Fey's Work
95 Critical Reviews
98 Timeline

101 Glossary
103 For More Information
106 For Further Reading
108 Bibliography
110 Index

INTRODUCTION

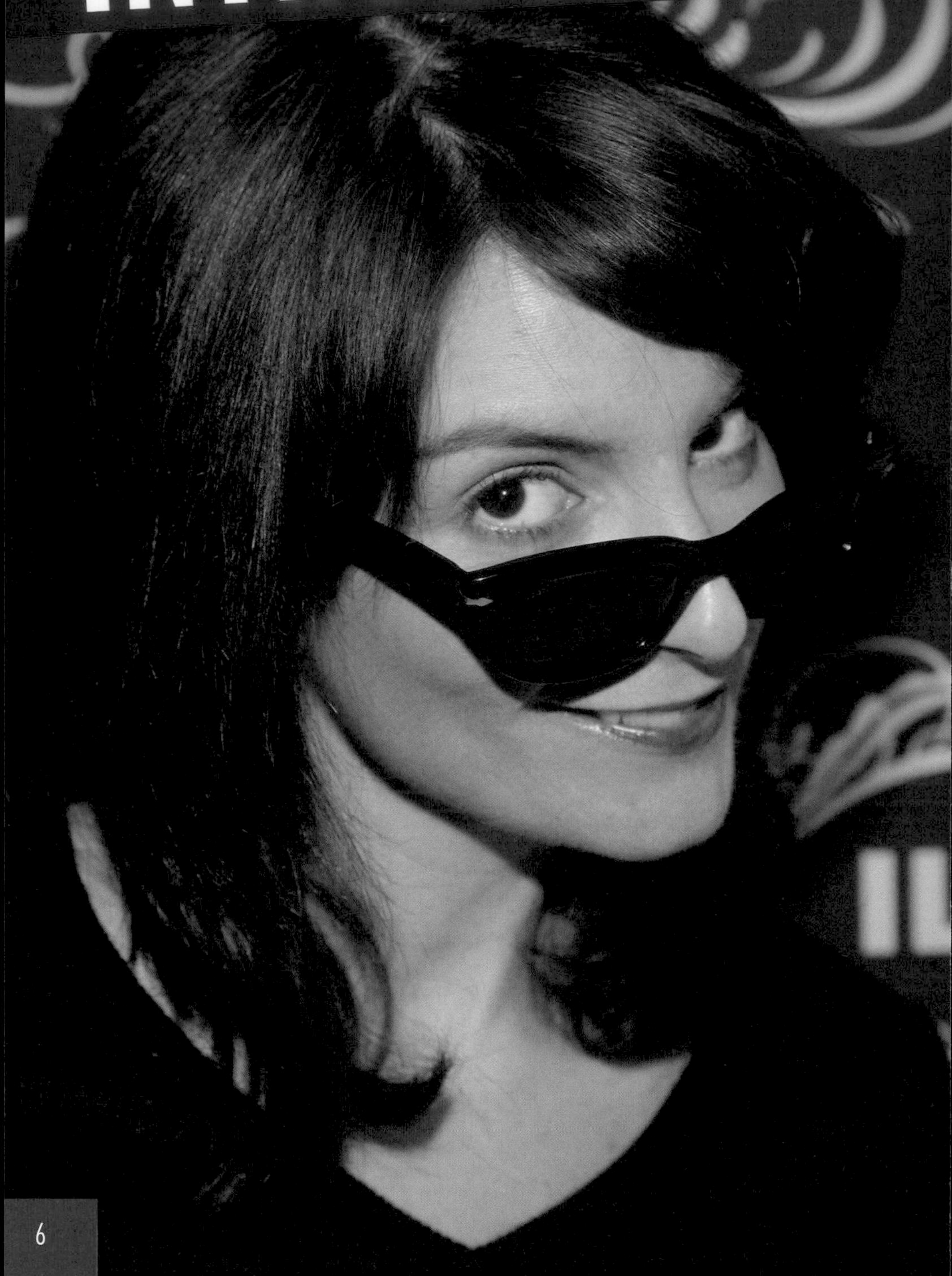

It would be nearly impossible to think of a more influential woman in modern comedy than the illustrious, ever-surprising Tina Fey.

Some may know her best as a long-running cast member and writer on *Saturday Night Live*, where she kept America in stitches as the beloved coanchor of the "Weekend Update" segment (and where she brought the house down with her impression of politician Sarah Palin). Others may know her as the creator of *Mean Girls*, the incredibly influential 2004 comedy that delivered a dark—and hilarious—perspective on the female high school experience. And still others are fans of Fey's madcap cult favorite *30 Rock*, a bold sit-com that sharply satirized the television industry.

Because of all that fame, you might imagine that Tina Fey was born into a legacy of stardom, a showbiz kid like Jaden Smith or Rumer Willis. Nothing could be further from the truth, though. As the child of an office worker mom and grant

Tina Fey's name has come to be synonymous with witty comedy. She is known for pushing the boundaries of women's roles in Hollywood.

writer dad in the decidedly unglamorous Upper Darby, Pennsylvania, Fey is the definition of a self-made star.

In a world where so many rich and famous people come from privileged backgrounds, it's refreshing to encounter a star with such modest roots. Just a regular girl—with a fierce sense of humor, of course—Fey is well-equipped to inspire legions of aspiring young comedians who are overwhelmed by the obstacles to success.

In particular, Fey is a solid role model for female comics in a field where men have traditionally held much of the power. Fey and her contemporary Amy Poehler have done an incredible job busting through gender barriers, providing a tough, unapologetic voice for women in comedy. This is partially circumstantial; Fey never stated an explicit goal to be some kind of feminist trailblazer. Yet she has recognized inequality when she encountered it—like at *Saturday Night Live*'s long-standing boy's club—and worked to change the status quo.

Fey is also a master of shrugging off her critics. Virtually anyone who has struggled to make it in entertainment has faced their share of doubters and naysayers. Listening to these voices is a quick path to self-doubt and modified dreams. But Fey understood from an early age that it's more important to listen to your inner voice than the jealous and mean-spirited voices around you. She is particularly adept at turning the negativity into comic gold for the benefit of her audience.

Fey is only in her forites now, yet her comic legacy is all but assured. Already numerous up-and-comers have cited her as a major influence. And while new generations of female and male comedians will come and go, one thing is certain—they will owe a debt of gratitude to Tina Fey for blazing new trails and reshifting the face of comedy today.

CHAPTER **ONE**

Back to the Roots

On May 18, 1970, Tina Fey was born Elizabeth Stamatina Fey; "Tina" was the short form of her Greek middle name. She grew up in the unremarkable town of Upper Darby, Pennsylvania, very similar to thousands of American suburbs. Situated west of Philadelphia, it's what some might call a "bedroom community"—most people who sleep in Upper Darby work in Philadelphia during the day.

Family Life

Tina's parents certainly fit the mold typical of their community. Her mother Zenobia "Jeanne," the child of Greek immigrant parents, was a homemaker and office worker at a Philadelphia brokerage firm. Her father, Donald Henry Fey, was the main breadwinner; he wrote grants at a local university.

10

Tina Fey grew up in Upper Darby, Pennsylvania, a suburb of Philadelphia. Upper Darby is a small town, covering just under 8 square miles (20.5 square km). Here, you can see the skyline of Philadelphia in the background.

One of the most remarkable things about Tina's childhood is how unremarkable it was in many ways. Her childhood was not marred by scandal and neglect, the kind that drives some artists to strengthen their resolve to overcome challenges. Conversely, she was not born with a silver spoon in her mouth; her family was staunchly middle-class, without any particular advantages to offer an aspiring comedian.

One thing Tina never lacked, however, was attention. Her brother, Peter, is eight years older than her, old enough to remove the competitive drive often found between siblings. Instead, Peter doted on her. In her memoir-meets-humor book, *Bossypants*, Tina says he looked after her "like a third parent."

Tina's parents, too, were dedicated to making sure she was well cared for. Her mother had Tina when she was forty years old, an uncommon occurrence back in 1970. This pregnancy was a late-in-life surprise, but not an unwelcome one. Her mother's coworkers referred to her as "Mrs. Fey's change of life baby."

Tina notes that, growing up, her parents were somewhat older than those of her peers. In *Bossypants*, she recounts a tale of showing up to kindergarten with a blanket for naptime with her initials stitched into it. When the teacher said, "We don't do that anymore," Tina said she was startled by the early realization that she had old parents.

But being older didn't mean that they were irrelevant, especially with regards to comedy. Tina's parents loved to laugh, and they influenced her with their own comedic tastes early on. Some of the most influential comedies she was exposed to as a kid include the zany Gene Wilder comedy *Young Frankenstein*, old black-and-white Marx Brothers slapstick films, and the madcap domestic sitcom

The Honeymooners. She also watched *Saturday Night Live* (foreshadowing her career to come), but one thing she never watched? *The Flintstones*. Her father said it was a *Honeymooners* ripoff; it was forbidden viewing in her household.

FEY'S FAVORITE CHILDHOOD TV SHOWS

It may not be surprising to learn that some of Tina Fey's favorite television shows when she was growing up were comedies. The influence of these programs is evident in some of the projects she would go on to pursue as an adult.

The Honeymooners: *The Honeymooners* was a working-class sitcom from the 1950s, focused on the dysfunctional marriage between bus driver Ralph Kramden and his wife, Alice. The show was (and is) wildly popular, despite the unflattering portrayal of women and Kramden's frequent threats of violence.

The Mary Tyler Moore Show: This Emmy-award-winning comedy centered around the workplace hijinks

(continued on the next page)

13

(continued from the previous page)

The cast of *The Mary Tyler Moore Show* poses on set in 1975. Pictured are: (*left to right*) Betty White, Ted Knight, Georgia Engel, Gavin McLeod, Mary Tyler Moore, and Ed Asner.

of an unmarried career woman in her thirties. The show's star plays a television producer; critics have drawn comparisons between *The Mary Tyler Moore Show* and *30 Rock* (Tina Fey's sitcom about an unmarried television producer named Liz Lemon).

Laverne and Shirley: This is another comedy focused on career women, in this case workers at a Milwaukee brewery. There is a madcap energy to this show, not dissimilar to the feeling on *30 Rock*.

The Bob Newhart Show: The soft-spoken comedian Bob Newhart actually had two sitcoms and one comedy variety show named after him. Fey has said in interviews she was a fan of both sitcoms. Newhart was known for his subtle delivery of scathing satire, so it's not hard to see why she enjoyed his style.

Saturday Night Live: Like many aspiring comedians in the last part of the twentieth century, Fey was a huge childhood fan of the sketch comedy show *Saturday Night Live.* However, unlike many of them, she would later get to live her dream of writing and performing on the show.

Growing up, Tina's father had a profound influence on her character. She dedicates an entire chapter of *Bossypants* to memories of him. The chapter is titled "That's Don Fey" because she actually heard two young women whispering that to each other when he walked by. Tina paints him as something of a minor celebrity, handsome and charming and impeccably dressed. She stood in awe of his many talents but also feared his disapproval. "How can I give [my daughter] what he gave me?" Tina writes. "The gift of anxiety. The fear of getting in trouble. The knowledge that while you are loved, you are not above the law."

Like many sons and daughters, Tina has complicated feelings about her dad (this might be true about her mother, too, but she talks about her less to the public). A Korean War veteran and former

Philadelphia firefighter, Don Fey was a strict man with big expectations of his daughter. His two favorite words were "inexcusable" (for grammar mistakes and being unobservant) and "defective" (for when something didn't work because he hadn't read the directions). It's clear he was firm but fair, teaching his daughter about a lack of self-importance, for which Tina gives him credit. About child raising, Tina says kids already think they're the most important people in the world and suggests that teaching them the opposite—that they are not perfect and must deal with the consequences of mistakes and misdeeds—is far more valuable. Through her writing, both for television and in her book, it is clear that Tina Fey was taught humility as well as sass from her father—and perhaps most importantly, that a strong character will always prevail.

An Early Trauma

Tina Fey has a scar along the left side of her face. It runs from the middle of her cheek to her chin. While it isn't obvious, it is easy to see when she smiles, which she does a lot. The scar is a remnant of a violent attack that happened in her front yard when she was five years old. Apparently, a man approached her and slashed her face with a knife. She recovered, but the long scar has remained with her ever since.

Tina remained quiet on the subject of her scar for many years. A highly private person, she didn't feel it was anyone's business. But, in 2008, she finally revealed that she'd been attacked as a child.

The way people react to it has provided Fey with entertainment and insight into the human psyche throughout her life. Some people actively ignore it, while others make assumptions about her attacker. Others outright ask her about it, seemingly patting themselves on the back for being so brave and understanding. During her years on *30 Rock*, the right side of her face was shown on camera more often than her left side.

But over the years, Fey has come to terms with it. She recalls being a confident child despite the scar, but she rarely mentions it in public and refuses to give very many details about the attack. She doesn't hide her face as much as she used to, even posing for glamorous magazines such as *Marie Claire* and *Vanity Fair*. But her therapist has warned her that she might be anxious about letting her daughters outside, the psychological remnants of a brutal attack that she has survived and overcome.

Early Education

Tina Fey attended Cardington-Stonehurst Elementary School in Upper Darby, Pennsylvania, followed by Beverly Hills Middle School. But it was at Upper Darby High School that Fey clearly began to find her footing.

At Upper Darby High Schoool Tina was not only an honors student, but a member of the school choir and the drama club, and she played tennis. But it was as an editor for her school's newspaper, that her wit and talent for comedy became clear. She anonymously wrote a satirical column for the newspaper under the nom de plume "The Colonel." The *Philadelphia Weekly* recounts one 1987 column in which the Colonel reacts to that year's homecoming king and queen: "And so out came the Homecoming Court. The Colonel was outraged ... There they stood on the platform, gloating over the prize that was rightfully the Colonel's. He saw the voting tab." Even at a young age, Tina's comic instinct was sharply tuned.

Fey openly admits that her high school experience influenced the characters and plot of her 2004 hit *Mean Girls*. The movie depicts the cruel things that high school students—and in particular, high school girls—can say and do to each other. She has reflected on her own experiences, in which girls threatened her or made vicious comments to her. Indirectly, she sometimes also engaged in such behavior herself. Fey told the *New York Times* that she thinks that some of her comedy in high school was partially fueled by the hostility she felt, saying, "I think I was playing offense a little bit. Like to a guy friend, I'd say: 'Really? That's who you like?' I would try to control people through shame. I only learned how to stop doing that like two years ago." When she remembers these experiences now, she can see how damaging such behavior is. As she says in *Mean Girls*, in *Bossypants*, and in many interviews that she's given: girl-on-girl sabotage is one of the worst things a woman can do.

FAMOUS FACES FROM PENNSYLVANIA

Pennsylvania, the sixth most populous state in the United States, is the birthplace of many famous contemporary entertainers. This is a list of a few of the actors, singers, and comedians who have called Pennsylvania home.

Christina Aguilera: The legendary pop vocalist, known for hits such as "Genie in a Bottle," "Lady Marmalade," and "Reflection" (from the Disney film *Mulan*), and for being a coach on *The Voice,* calls her hometown(s) Rochester and Wexford, Pennsylvania.

Bradley Cooper: The actor best known for *The Hangover* (2009), *Silver Linings Playbook* (2012), and *American Sniper* (2014) was born in Philadelphia and raised in neighboring towns.

Seth Green: The actor and director known for television programs such as *Buffy the Vampire Slayer,*

Family Guy, and *Robot Chicken* is from Overbrook Park in West Philadelphia.

Kevin Hart: The actor and stand-up comedian best known for *Scary Movie 3* (2003), *The 40-Year-Old Virgin* (2005), and *Ride Along* (2014) was born in North Philadelphia.

Pink (Alecia Moore): The pop singer, whose hits include "Get The Party Started" and "Just Give Me a Reason," is from Reading.

M. Night Shyamalan: The screenwriter, director, producer, and occasional actor known for films such as *The Sixth Sense* (1999), *Signs* (2002), *The Village* (2004), and *The Visit* (2015) hails from Willistown.

Will Smith: The famous actor and rapper and patriarch of the Pinkett-Smith clan is from Philadelphia. As he proudly proclaims: "In West Philadelphia, born and raised."

Taylor Swift: The businesswoman, actress, and singer/songwriter best known for her songs about teenage heartbreak such as "Our Song," "Romeo and Juliet," and "You Belong with Me," grew up in Reading and Wyomissing before moving to Tennessee.

Upper Darby Summer Stage

One of the brighter aspects of Tina's high school life was her involvement with the Upper Darby High School's Summer Stage (a program she enigmatically refers to in *Bossypants* as the Delaware County Summer Showtime). Each summer the program brings together young adults and college students and grads to put on different kinds of staged performances, from children's musicals to Broadway shows. A self-proclaimed nerd and a rather lonely and awkward teen, this became her favorite summer activity.

The program not only exposed local children to live theater, it involved the entire community. Teens, middle-school students, and adults alike worked together on creating costumes and sets, directing, perfecting the lighting, and putting on several productions over the course of the summer. Tina had stints working in the box office, writing press releases, acting, and directing plays. She wrote skits that teased kids involved in Summer Stage (a tradition staff members participated in each summer) in which she came up with memorable zingers. She also had the chance to do some improv (short for improvisational) acting—that is, unrehearsed performances made up on the spot—something she would come back to later in her career.

It was during the summers she spent working at the Summer Stage that Tina encountered her first heartbreak over a boy, met her first gay friends—who helped shape her own understanding of homosexuality and gay marriage—and had her first real experience with a theater family. Summer Stage gave Tina the early tools with which she would spend the rest of her life navigating the stage and the real world. Even after she became a celebrity, Fey would remain a strong supporter of the program.

CHAPTER
TWO

Finding Herself

Fey graduated from Upper Darby High School in 1988, and in the fall of that year she began attending college at the University of Virginia, where she studied playwriting and acting. She described herself as looking "Mexican" in comparison to her blond and blue-eyed classmates—many of whom seemed to come from privilege (she has said that many owned horses or "resembled them").

She was an outsider in Virginia, attending the college founded by Thomas Jefferson. Simply called "Virginia" by locals and students, it is known for its historic foundations, student-run honor committee, and secret organizations—of which Fey was absolutely not a part.

Instead, she preferred the drama department, putting on such productions as *The Robber Bridegroom* and going to cast parties rather

Thomas Jefferson founded the University of Virginia in 1819, in Charlottesville, Virginia. A statue of the third president of the United States stands in front of the university's most iconic building, the Rotunda.

than fraternity parties. She watched *Saturday Night Live* in her dorm room and studied hard. Though studious, she was eager to have a few more life experiences, as well.

Disastrous Dates

Although for many people college is a time of sexual experimentation, Fey says that this was definitely not the case for her. "I spent four years attempting to charm the uninterested," she says in *Bossypants*. Though she tried very hard, she felt she wasn't white enough or exotic-looking enough to attract attention from the young men at UVA.

She did catch the attention of one young man who was clearly using her for her eager companionship. He never took her out on dates, except to the mall to help him pick out presents for other girls. She did, however, climb Old Crag Mountain in the Blue Ridge Mountains for him one night, in hopes of advancing the relationship. He brought his roommate, however, and neither boy brought flashlights or water. Her "date" fell off the mountain while he was showing off, but, thankfully wasn't seriously injured. At the top of the mountain, he told Fey about his love for another girl.

Although she was a typical, hormone-driven college student, Fey admits she was "terrified" at the thought of having sex. She knew that it wasn't something she was ready for, emotionally or physically. Instead, she focused on other pursuits. She proudly claims that she was an "achievement-oriented, obedient, drug-free, virgin adult."

The impact of such experiences is evident in Fey's later comedy. Her characters are often awkward and even uncomfortable around the opposite sex. Her sketches on *Saturday Night Live* were often parodies of awkward women and girls. And on *30 Rock*, the protagonist Liz Lemon, portrayed by Fey, is extremely socially awkward and uncomfortable with men, especially when becoming intimate with them. And while these are funny to watch, they also seem to mirror her early experiences with the opposite sex.

Fey graduated from the University of Virginia in 1992 with a bachelor of arts in drama, and on Halloween of the following year moved to Chicago, excited to see what opportunities a new city might offer her.

Chicago

After applying for jobs as a waitress, the night box office manager of a small theater company in the Boystown neighborhood of Chicago, and a receptionist at a lawyer's office (who was a friend of her mother's), Fey finally got a job working the front desk of the Evanston (a suburb of Chicago) YMCA. She worked the shift from 5:30 a.m. to 2:30 p.m., which gave her plenty of time for auditions, rehearsals, and improv classes.

Many of the residents and coworkers she encountered in this position would inspire characters for her sketches for years to come. Some such individuals included drifters with untrimmed fingernails and dirty underwear who tried to sneak women up to their rooms while wearing large overcoats and hats. A redhead who worked the phones and complained constantly and a lisping mail-sorting man were also fixtures in her day-to-day routine. Fey claims it was just like a sitcom—only missing the studio audience and the big salaries. One quality Fey gained from working at the Evanston YMCA was her ability to be a considerate coworker, something that would come in handy later when working in television and supervising a large number of different personality types. Like her childhood in the Fey household, working at the YMCA taught Tina some humility and appreciation. Seeing men with so little that they were happy to get tube socks for Christmas and a vending machine sandwich for dinner made her sad but also grateful for everything she already had in her life: her mind, her family, and her ambition. That ambition drove her from the front desk to a job in the office upstairs at the YMCA, where

EARLY JOBS FOR COMEDIANS

Comedy can be a very difficult career field to break into. Like Fey, a number of famous comedians and comedic actors worked in a variety of occupations before catching their big break. In some cases, these early experiences even shaped their comedy.

Drew Carey was a waiter at a Denny's in his hometown of Cleveland, Ohio.

Jim Carrey was a factory cleaner after he dropped out of high school at fifteen to help support his family.

Louis C. K. was a car mechanic before starting his stand-up and television career, although he debated going to law school.

Dane Cook worked at Burger King and was a newspaper delivery boy.

Ellen Degeneres was a door-to-door vacuum salesperson (interestingly enough, so was Willie Nelson!).

Danny DeVito was a hairdresser.

Jim Gaffigan studied finance and originally moved to New York to work in advertising.

Zach Galifianakis was a bus boy in a strip club in New York.

Whoopi Goldberg was a mortuary cosmetician, applying makeup to dead people before their open-casket funerals.

Kevin Hart sold sneakers and almost went to work for Nike before catching the comedy bug.

(continued on the next page)

(continued from the previous page)

Gabriel Iglesias sold cell phones before beginning his stand-up career.

Jerry Seinfeld sold lightbulbs before redefining the television sitcom in the 1990s.

Jon Stewart was a puppeteer on a program for disabled children before he began his sixteen-year tenure as host of the *Daily Show.*

she worked until she got the opportunity that would change her life.

The Second City

In 1994, Tina Fey was offered the chance of a lifetime: she was cast as a member of the Second City comedy troupe in Chicago. Second City is a famed comedy institution, noted for its robust programs in improv and sketch comedy (unlike improv, sketch comedy is scripted and can involve the use of props, sets, and costumes). It has been in operation continuously since 1959, beginning on the campus of the University of Chicago in the 1950s. On December 16, 1959, the group opened a theater in Chicago and has been growing ever since. Fey went on the road with Second City,

This photo from around 1976 shows *SCTV* cast members John Candy (*top*), Joe Flaherty (*middle row, left*), Andrea Martin, Rick Moranis, Catherine O'Hara, Dave Thomas (*bottom left*), and Eugene Levy.

touring with such future comedy stars as Amy Poehler.

From one small theater and a group of less than a dozen actors, Second City has grown to include multiple resident companies that perform in sold-out shows in Chicago, Toronto, and Los Angeles. There are also three touring companies that take the best sketches on the road to cities across North America.

Now, Second City sponsors not only the resident companies and touring companies in each of their host cities (Chicago, Toronto, and Los Angeles), but it also has a company dedicated solely to the purpose of outreach and education.

Second City even had its own television show, a sketch comedy called *SCTV*, which ran from 1976–84. The premise was very simple: a small-town TV station in fictional Melonville, USA, is run by the greedy Guy Caballero, who feigns needing a wheelchair for sympathy. Instead of running expensive programming, he decides to showcase cheaper, locally made television shows. Some of these shows included a soap opera called *The Days of the Week*; a game show entitled *Shoot At the Stars*, in which comedians would impersonate celebrities who were literally being used for target practice; and many movie spoofs. Martin Short originated his *Saturday Night Live* character of Ed Grimley on

SCTV. Many other Second City alums went on to become *Saturday Night Live* cast members as well.

After years of taking improv classes, it seemed that Fey had found her calling as a comedian. She loves the concept of improv theater more than that of sketch comedy: actors on stage create some- thing together spur-of-the moment—with no script or set or costume for inspiration—that is completely authentic and unique for that audience alone.

There are various rules for improv theater. Three important ones are:

1. Yes and agree: No matter what your scene partner says or does, you must go with it. If he/ she states "This room is so blue!," it is much bet- ter to respond with "Well of course, we're inside Poseidon's castle" than to reply with "No it's not. It's red." Even if it is in fact, red. This rule goes hand- in-hand with "Yes and," meaning you must add to whatever your scene partner has previously stated. Simply agreeing is not enough. A scene will become stagnant if two partners are not constantly adding on to what the other has said.

2. Make statements: Asking questions will only put one scene partner in the position of having to come up with all the information and scenery him or herself. "Where are we?" does little for a scene.

"We're floating on a cloud above Mount Vesuvius as it erupts" does a bit more to move a scene forward.

3. There are no mistakes: Even if one scene partner is convinced he or she is riding a trolley, the other partner might see you as conducting a train. And once your partner has said "Why, Mr. Conductor, why are you pulling at the whistle so hard?" in front of a live audience, there is no taking it back. And so, even though it might be considered a mistake, the two actors must roll with the punches and drive the scene forward.

FAMOUS SECOND CITY ALUMS

Numerous comedians and comedic actors and *Saturday Night Live* cast members got their start at Second City. The following is a list of some Second City alums who have gone on to have successful careers in television and film.

Dan Aykroyd is an actor, comedian, and musician best known for films like *The Blues Brothers* (1980), *Ghostbusters* (1984), *Driving Miss Daisy* (1989), and ,of course, his years as a cast member on *Saturday Night Live* (1975–79).

Perhaps two of the most notable Second City Alums in recent history are Stephen Colbert (*left*) and Steve Carrell. Here, the two speak at the 2014 Montclair Film Festival.

Steve Carrell is a former *The Daily Show* correspondent who went on to play Michael Scott on the American version of the television show *The Office* (2005–11). His film credits include *Bruce Almighty* (2003), its sequel *Evan Almighty* (2007), *Anchorman* (2004), *The 40-Year-Old Virgin* (2005), *Little Miss Sunshine* (2006), and *Despicable Me* (2010).

Stephen Colbert is an actor, comedian, producer, and television host who is probably best known for his late-night work on *The Daily Show* (1997–2005) and

(continued on the next page)

(continued from the previous page)

The Colbert Report (2005–14). He took over for David Letterman as host of *The Late Show* in September 2015.

Catherine O'Hara is one of Tina Fey's idols. She started her career on *SCTV.* She's well recognized for such films as *Beetlejuice* (1988), *Home Alone* (1990), *Lemony Snicket's A Series of Unfortunate Events* (2004), and television shows such as *Six Feet Under* (2003–05). In 2012 she worked with Tina Fey on *30 Rock.*

Amy Poehler worked with Fey at Second City, and she was also on *Saturday Night Live* from 2001–08. Her television sitcom *Parks and Recreation* (2009–15) won several Emmys. She also cohosted the seventieth, seventy-first, and seventy-second Golden Globe Awards with Tina Fey. These attracted the program's highest viewership in recent history. Her best known films are *Wet, Hot American Summer* (2001), *Mean Girls* (2004, with Fey), *Baby Mama* (2008, also with Fey), and *Inside Out* (2015). She and Fey reunited again for *Sisters* (2015).

Martin Short is an actor, singer, comedian and pro-ducer, probably best known for his films *¡Three Amigos!* (1986), *Father of the Bride* (1991), and *Jungle 2 Jungle* (1997). His television appearances include *How I Met Your Mother* and *Unbreakable Kimmy Schmidt.* He was a cast member on *Saturday Night Live* from 1984–85.

The idea of improvisational comedy is very simple: two (or more) actors must work together using only their wits to create an entertaining scene from nothing. Sometimes they fall flat. And other times, they become legendary.

On the Road with Second City

Fey began her time at Second City as a member of one of the three touring groups. These groups tour the country and perform the Second City's most popular sketches. Each company has a name: Red Company, Green Company, and Blue Company. Fey was a member of the Blue Company, or BlueCo as she and Poehler called it.

They toured the United States in a van going from city to city, getting paid $75 for each performance, plus $25 per diem. (Per diem is often what companies will pay for daily living expenses such as food, lodging, and gas.) Cramped in a van with four men and one other woman, Fey dreamed of becoming a part of one of the Mainstage companies, which would allow her to stay in Chicago and earn a livable, unionized wage.

Fey toured with Amy Poehler during her first year with Second City, going to places such as upstate New York; St. Paul, Minnesota; Waco, Texas; and Kansas. They performed at after parties for high school proms (which occurred after prom and were designed to keep teenagers from getting into trouble), corporate retreats, and other such events where the audiences were less than thrilled to be seeing a comedy show.

But Fey (and Poehler) would not be deterred. They even went off-script—or at least as off-script as sketch comedy could be—performing their own material instead of the preapproved sketches determined by Second City producers. This, it seems, is where Fey got her sea legs in comedy. She learned all the "rules" of improv and began her illustrious writing career. She was in love with the way improv worked, the people she met, and being a part of something bigger than herself. "Studying improvisation literally changed my life...It changed the way I look at the world," she writes in *Bossypants*.

Important Relationships

At the Second City, Fey's love life finally turned around. She met and began dating her future husband, Jeff Richmond, a pianist and composer who was also working for the company. They bonded over a mutual love of hot veal sandwiches and sarcastic humor and became serious after spending a magical Sunday afternoon at the Museum of Science and Industry in Chicago. They have been inseparable ever since. This is one of a few significant relationships Fey developed during her time in Chicago.

Tina Fey and Amy Poehler have a well-documented decades-long friendship. Fey actually met Poehler before they began at Second City. They were both taking improv classes at the ImprovOlympic Theater (now known as the iO Theater) in Chicago in 1993. One of the cofounders of ImprovOlympic introduced them, thinking they would get along. She could not have been more right. Fey and Poehler hit it off immediately. They took classes at the theater, often sitting together at the back of a classroom exchanging jokes. The two fearless comedians performed a two-woman show there called *Women of Color*, which blended improv and sketch comedy. They both moved on to roles at the Second City. In 1996, when Poehler left Chicago—and her role as a Mainstage player at Second City—Fey would get her break and become a Mainstage player herself.

Despite Poehler's leaving the city, however, she and Fey remained close. They worked together on *Saturday Night Live*, as well as the film *Baby Mama* (2008), and most recently, *Sisters* (2015). Poehler says about Fey: "Tina and I don't have sisters [in real life]. We each have a brother. Tina is certainly my longest female relationship other than a few of my old childhood friends. She and I have been friends

Tina Fey and Rachel Dratch have been friends for many years, even creating a two-woman show together while working at *Saturday Night Live*.

for 20 years. She is my chosen sister." It's clear
the two know each other well. At the 2015 Golden
Globe awards, Fey joked that the two of them had
been friends for fifty years, stating that the secret
to their friendship is that they have no overlap in
their taste in men, even going on to play "Would You
Rather...?" on live television.

Another influential and long-lasting friendship
Fey made at Second City was with Rachel Dratch,
a comedian and writer whose face is well known to
comedy fans. In 1999, the two staged a two-woman
show (which Tina lovingly mocked on *30 Rock*),
called *Dratch & Fey*. The show appeared both at
Chicago's Second City as well as another famous
improv comedy theater, New York City's Upright
Citizen's Brigade. It was directed by Fey's future
husband, Jeff Richmond.

The show features both women poking fun at
society, poignantly pointing out some issues facing the modern woman, and, in general, having fun.
Part of the show was improvised, and part of it was
scripted. In one sketch, Dratch plays Edwina Garth
Turnham a fictional twentieth-century women's
rights pioneer while Fey portrays a modern woman
becoming more aware of and open about her sexu-
ality. In another sketch, a Learning Center teacher,
Alice Kinsella (played by Dratch), must combine

two classes because of low enrollment. These two classes are "Self Defense for Women" and "Intro to Flirting." Hilariously enough, Dratch deadpans the lines, saying both "no means no" and "no means maybe"—a funny and provocative take on the conflicting social messages directed at women.

Fey's comedy has always been thought-provoking and reflects many social issues that are facing society as a whole. She's never been afraid to discuss topics that others shy away from. Women's issues are an especially hot topic for Fey. Some of her *Saturday Night Live* sketches have mocked menstruation, or spinsters, or even how women are portrayed in the media. "It's funny because it's true," seems to describe Fey's style and the topics she chooses to discuss. Although both Dratch and Fey were on *Saturday Night Live* when they performed their two-woman show—Dratch as a cast member and Fey as a writer—their careers would go on to blow up as they had never anticipated.

CHAPTER
THREE

Saturday Night Live

In 1997, Fey got the opportunity she'd always dreamed of: she was called in to interview with Lorne Michaels, creator and producer of *Saturday Night Live (SNL)*, for a job as a writer on the show. As the name suggests, the show runs live many Saturday nights throughout the year, from 11:30 p.m. to 1:00 a.m. The show features a regular cast, and each week it has a different celebrity host. *SNL* debuted in 1975 and has been a late-night institution since, drawing numerous actors, comedians, athletes, politicians, and more to its stage. In 1997, the head writer was a former Second City performer who asked Fey to submit scripts for sketches on the show. She obliged and was later asked to meet with Michaels.

Fey had grown up watching the late-night sketch comedy show and was understandably nervous. She'd heard stories about Lorne

Michaels's stern demeanor and how he liked people to talk to him. Despite having broken a few of these "rules" in her interview, Fey landed the job.

Saturday Night Live's First Female Head Writer

In 1999, Tina was promoted to head writer, the first woman ever to hold this position. At the time, the sketch comedy show was trying to rebrand itself. Viewership was at an all-time low, and the staff was struggling to find a new (female) voice for the new millennium. Fey's best work seemed to be parodies: from a sketch starring Chris Farley making fun of daytime TV talk show *Sally* to one mocking *The View* to sketches lampooning many different politicians, actors, and celebrities.

As the first female writer of *SNL*, Tina Fey had to negotiate a virtual boys' world. Comedy writers had notoriously been men before then. A common phrase was "Women aren't funny." On late night television shows especially—including *SNL*—a female head writer was unheard of. All the late night talk show hosts were men (David Letterman, Jay Leno, Jon Stewart, etc.). And the most famous people to come off of *SNL* before Fey were cast members such as John Belushi, Eddie Murphy, Chevy Chase, Bill Murray, Dan Aykroyd, and Chris Farley, to name a few. Not that there hadn't been famous women on the show—Gilda Radner, Jane

Curtin, and Julia Louis-Dreyfus are just some of the many notable former female cast members. But Fey suddenly had to fill the shoes of such famous comedians in addition to creating a new voice for *SNL*. And she did. During Tina Fey's tenure at *SNL* famous comedians, both male and female, found fame. The careers of Kristin Wiig, Amy Poehler, Rachel Dratch, Will Forte, Seth Meyers, Fred Armisen, and Maya Rudolph all took off thanks to the "Tina Fey regime" on *SNL*. Moreover, Fey helped transform *SNL* culture from what former female cast members have described as "frat house" behavior into one in which women cast members have greater freedom of expression and in which women's issues are discussed in frank and sometimes explicit terms rather than being hidden or downplayed.

As a writer, Fey had to learn the ropes and stretch her comedic talents. Navigating the world of late night sketch comedy was challenging. There were late nights, quick meals (which sometimes consisted of potato chips and coffee), and long hours working on sets, costumes, scripts, and budgets. She recalls watching her sketches being performed from under the bleachers in the audience, holding her breath and waiting to see Lorne Michaels's reaction. She learned a lot from Michaels, including the fact that when a sketch "bombed" it wasn't the end of her career. Yes, she wrote some sketches that aren't so famous. But the ones that were successful have gone down in television (and Internet) history.

Historically, *SNL* writers and cast members have had particular types of backgrounds. Many were either stand-up comedians or writers/performers at Second City or other similar institutions, including the Groundlings improv troupe in Los Angeles, California. Harvard alums who worked for the Harvard humor magazine, the *Harvard Lampoon,* brought a third type of comedy sensibility. As Fey learned, mixing the quirky improvisers and stand-up comedians with the Ivy League writers helped balance the show's blend of humor. This formula resulted not only in a great stage cast, but a diverse and hilarious group of writers who shied away from nothing. Fey parodies this on *30 Rock* and talks about it at length in *Bossypants*. Lorne Michaels told Fey never to hire anyone she wouldn't want to run into at three o'clock in the morning. This seems a good rule of thumb in general.

Fey also learned a lot about working in television. She learned that producers have to be realistic, not just creative (budgets are set for a reason). She learned that television is a visual medium, so each performer should look his or her best on camera. This may seem obvious, but when Fey worked

In 2002, Fey won the Primetime Emmy Award for Outstanding Writing for a Variety, Music, or Comedy program for her work on *Saturday Night Live*. She would continue to win awards and accolades for her writing.

as head writer, there were long nights, which made her look tired. Michaels had seen a performance of *Dratch & Fey* and wanted Fey to perform onscreen, in addition to continuing as a writer. Fey appeared in a sketch, saw herself afterward, and was appalled. She found that she looked heavy on screen, much larger than she'd ever considered herself. But those late nights and bad meals had caught up with her. So, she began dieting and exercising and lost 30 pounds (13 kg). In 2000, she donned her now signature black-rimmed glasses and became a regular coanchor of *Saturday Night Live*'s "Weekend Update" with Jimmy Fallon while also appearing in other sketches.

FEY'S BEST-KNOWN *SNL* SKETCHES

In addition to her writing accomplishments on *SNL*, Tina Fey also portrayed some pretty memorable characters while she was a full-time cast member. She also had some hilarious guest appearances after leaving the show in 2006. The following are some of her notable sketches.

"Mom Jeans" (2003): In this prefilmed mock ad, Fey, Poehler, Dratch, and Maya Rudolph portray mothers who, because they spend so much time looking after their families and working, wear the comfortable—but unattractive—"Mom jeans." These jeans come in different (and equally unflattering) styles. The hilarious ad was also a commentary on the often unfair media portrayal of women who have had children.

Tina Fey and Amy Poehler as the Bush twins (2005): In this sketch, Fey and Poehler played the twin daughters of President George W. Bush talking to each other the night of their father's second inaugural ball. Clueless and hilarious, they speak in their own "secret twin language," which consists of nothing more than placing a "buh" before each syllable: "buh-But buh-what buh-about buh-the buh-weapons of buh-mass buh-destruction?"

"Lady Business" (2008): Parodying television shows such as *Sex and the City, Cashmere Mafia*, and *Lipstick Jungle*, which centered on successful women living in big cities, Fey played a friend of similarly successful women. Instead of a glamorous, high paying job, however, Fey's character removes dead animals from underneath people's houses with either a vacuum or a hook.

Sarah Palin (2008): Over much of the 2008 season, Tina Fey famously appeared on *SNL* as vice presidential candidate Sarah Palin. Her spot-on impersonation (down to the similar glasses both women are known for wearing) and ability to cleverly convey important ideas about issues such as sexism helped boost the viewership of *30 Rock*. Sarah Palin herself even appeared in one sketch.

(continued on the next page)

(continued from the previous page)

"Mother's Message" (2011): In the show's Mother's Day special, Tina Fey (six months pregnant with her second child at the time), performed a song with another pregnant *SNL* alum, Maya Rudolph. At first, it is a sweet song where the two comedians talk to their unborn children. It ends with the two of them informing their babies that they are proof of their parents "doing it."

Girls parody: While hosting *SNL* in 2013, Fey did a memorable spoof of the HBO show *Girls*, in which she played a new girl to the crew—an immigrant from Albania named Blerta. Blerta has a rubber hand, wears traditional Albanian clothes, and doesn't understand the main characters' lives in New York City.

"Weekend Update"

In 2000, Tina Fey was offered the job as coanchor (with Jimmy Fallon) of "Weekend Update," a segment on the weekly show that highlights stories from the news with a humorous twist. Lorne Michaels determined that the two had chemistry and would do well in the segment, which had been falling flat with viewers.

Fey and Fallon rejuvenated the segment, breathing new life into it. Fey's ability to stay stone-faced

"Weekend Update" made Tina Fey a household name and a highly recognizable face. In this still from the show in 2003, Tina Fey and Jimmy Fallon are clearly having fun behind the "Weekend Update" desk.

despite whatever she was saying, her witty, quick one-liners, and her welcoming, down-to-earth look provided audiences with a relatable, hilarious anchor.

They made the segment legendary and a highly anticipated part of each episode of *SNL*. In 2004, after Fallon left *SNL*, Amy Poehler took over as co-anchor. Fey and Poehler were the first—and, to date, only—female anchor team on the show. After Fey

After Jimmy Fallon left *SNL*, Amy Poehler took over as coanchor of "Weekend Update" with Tina Fey. The two women would continue to create legendary comedy moments throughout their tenures on *Saturday Night Live*.

retired as a writer and cast member in 2006 to focus on her sitcom *30 Rock*, Seth Meyers (now host of *Late Night*) took over the coanchor role for Fey.

The Sketch Seen 'Round the World

During the 2008 presidential race, Republican candidate John McCain announced relatively unknown Alaska Governor Sarah Palin as his running mate. Unprepared for the media madness, Palin was known for making ill-advised comments and for

coming across as unprepared and unknowledge-
able in interviews. In addition to her rather laughable
media presence, Palin is also known for her physical
resemblance to Tina Fey.

On September 13, 2008, during the opening
monologue of the season premiere of *SNL*, Amy
Poehler and Tina Fey starred in and wrote a sketch
titled "A Nonpartisan Message from Governor Sarah
Palin and Senator Hillary Clinton." It begins simply
enough, with the two women discussing the position
of women in politics. Palin (Fey) begins saying more
and more ridiculous things about the role of women,
while Clinton (Poehler) becomes more and more
appalled.

Although Fey was no longer a cast member, the
sketch was so popular that she appeared multiple
times throughout the season, impersonating Palin in
such an accurate way sometimes it was difficult to
tell the two apart. Fey appeared in parodies of interviews (including a famous interview Palin did with
Katie Couric, portrayed by Poehler in the sketch)
and press conferences and portrayed Palin in other
fictional television appearances.

As the campaign continued, Palin continued to
flub interviews and jokingly claimed she was giving
Fey more material. In fact, Palin loved the parody,
saying that the physical resemblance was spot-
on and that the others on her campaign watched

As the 2008 presidential race heated up, Fey brilliantly portrayed Alaska governor Sarah Palin alongside Amy Poehler's Hillary Clinton. The sketch shot Tina Fey into comedy superstardom.

the videos over and over, laughing late into the night. Palin even claimed she dressed as Fey for Halloween. In the October 18, 2008, episode of *Saturday Night Live*, Palin even made an appearance in a sketch alongside Tina Fey for the cold opening.

Fey's portrayal of Palin reflected many of the issues facing Americans during that campaign, particularly those facing women. The role of women in politics has always been a hot topic of discussion. In many cases, women in powerful roles have been criticized for either being heartless and mean or for pandering to the lowest common denominator and being less intelligent than their male counterparts. Palin and Hillary Clinton seemed to epitomize these different stereotypes. Palin often did seem to pander to her audience, and Clinton has a reputation for being hard and cold. Neither woman has been able to successfully shake these public opinions in the years since.

Although Fey was no longer on the show, her portrayal of the governor attracted many viewers. As the videos hit the Internet, it seemed the world was abuzz about Fey, shooting her into superstardom. Ratings of *30 Rock* skyrocketed, and Fey was offered a book deal. Tina Fey had become a household name, a recognizable face, and a respected creator in comedy. Fey hosted *SNL* four times between 2008 and 2013 (winning Emmy nominations for two of them), but her Palin impersonations remain among her most popular appearances on the show.

CHAPTER
FOUR

30 Rock

It is clear to anyone who has ever seen *30 Rock* that the show is largely based on Fey's experiences writing and working on *Saturday Night Live*. The show centers around the head writer (Fey) of a live sketch comedy show originally titled *The Girlie Show* (*TGS*), which stars a female lead, Jenna Maroney (played by Jane Krakowski). The set is located at 30 Rockefeller Plaza (referred to locally as 30 Rock), where *Saturday Night Live* is actually taped and written (along with many other live television shows). When NBC is bought by GE (General Electric), the new executive, Jack Donaghy (Alec Baldwin), tries to revamp the show by casting a notoriously odd and eccentric stand-up comedian, Tracy Jordan (Tracy Morgan). Through seven seasons, the sitcom introduces its audience to the characters that create *TGS*: the writers, the cast members, and staff.

The show-within-a-show gives audiences a behind-the-scenes satirical and humorous view of what it's like to work in television. It also holds up a mirror to society and makes its viewers think, even as it makes them laugh.

The Beginnings of *30 Rock*

Back when Fey was the head writer on *SNL*, she pitched a situation comedy series about cable news to NBC. It was rejected. Producers felt that Fey was trying too hard, and they suggested she write about what she knew.

What Fey knew best was sketch comedy. So she rewrote the sitcom to revolve around an *SNL*-like comedy show. In 2004, a pilot for the *Untitled Tina Fey Project* was announced. Originally, the pilot was supposed to focus on the head writer of a variety show who navigated complicated work relationships with the show's unpredictable star—to be played by Rachel Dratch—and its charming executive producer. After many rewrites, the show's premise changed to involve the head writer managing her writers, actors, budget, and her own personal life as well as those of the stars and the executive.

NBC bought the pilot and set it to air for the 2005–06 television season. However, that was Fey's final season on *SNL*, and NBC executives feared that her leaving the famous sketch comedy show would negatively affect ratings and viewership. Fey renewed her contract with NBC to stay on as head writer, while developing her own show on the side. Filming was postponed when Fey became pregnant. The sitcom made its debut on October 11, 2006. Interestingly, that same pilot season, another program about a sketch comedy show debuted on the same network. Although ostensibly about a comedy, that program, *Studio 60 on the Sunset Strip*, was a drama. The two shows had some similarities but were developed separately and the creators of each did not like having the shows compared. Ultimately, however, it seemed audiences were only ready for one show-within-a-show. *Studio 60* was canceled after just one season while *30 Rock* went on to run for seven seasons.

Production and the Cast of *30 Rock*

In spite of its name and apparent setting, the show was not actually filmed at 30 Rockefeller Plaza in New York City. Instead, all of its interior shots (meaning those that take place inside) were filmed at Silver Cup Studios, in Long Island City, Queens, where other well-known films and TV shows have been shot. All exterior shots were filmed on location in Manhattan.

The core cast of *30 Rock* largely drove the sitcom's success for seven seasons. The characters are well known to their fans and give an element to the show that was essential to its success. However, pulling the cast together was not a simple process. Fey wrote the role of the show's star specifically for her friend and former colleague Rachel Dratch. However, network executives felt that the show needed to take another approach. Ultimately, Dratch was replaced and only appeared in the show in various (memorable) cameos. Additionally, convincing Alec Baldwin to take the role of a charismatic GE executive who comes to NBC proved difficult. Fey had envisioned Baldwin as a key executive in her initial pitch for a show revolving around a cable news network and had tweaked that role when she reworked her pilot to revolve around sketch comedy. Although the actor had hosted *SNL* numerous times (and is one of the show's most frequent hosts), he was known for his roles in film and was reluctant to take on a recurring role on television. He also spoke of being nervous about taking on a comedic role in a show with writers and actors who had actually been trained in comedy (unlike himself). However, Baldwin's respect for Fey's writing and some convincing arguments from his friend Lorne Michaels ultimately prompted Baldwin to take the role. He would become one of the show's most important stars.

Tina Fey and Alec Baldwin had great chemistry on screen. The relationship between Liz Lemon and Jack Donaghy was one of the driving forces of the sitcom's plot. *30 Rock* earned both actors many accolades and awards.

If Baldwin was instrumental to the show's success, however, it was in large part because of his on-screen chemistry with the other cast members, especially Tina Fey herself. Fey plays Liz Lemon the head writer of *TGS*. The character is loosely based on Tina Fey. She is eccentric, nerdy, and obsessive/compulsive when it comes to work, but clueless in her personal life. Over seven seasons the audience sees Liz Lemon deal with multiple moral dilemmas, her growing role as a manager, several boyfriends, and her mentor-mentee relationship with Jack Donaghy (Baldwin). Liz Lemon is awkward, relatable, and a joy to watch grow.

Alec Baldwin plays Jack Donaghy, the wealthy GE/NBC executive who only looks at the bottom line. Jack's character becomes Liz Lemon's mentor over the course of the show, guiding her to her full management potential. They become good friends and confidantes. His character is often used to show class issues in both show business and society. He is an elitist with a lot of money who is often out of touch with his coworkers, as well as with his audience. His heart is always in it for business, but he proves to be capable of adaptation and even grows to become fond of Liz Lemon and *TGS*.

Jane Krakowski plays Jenna Maroney, a stereotypically high-maintenance actress obsessed with getting her time in the spotlight. Her relationship with Liz is loosely based on that between Fey and Rachel Dratch. Like the real-life friends, Liz Lemon and Jenna Maroney lived in Chicago before coming to New York and did a two-woman show together. Maroney'a character (along with Liz Lemon) is often used to showcase issues in women's equality, most

In 2011, *30 Rock* celebrated one hundred episodes. Tina Fey, Alec Baldwin, Jane Krakowski (right of Baldwin), Tracy Morgan (far right), and Jack McBrayer (left of Fey), pose with the rest of the cast.

notably aging, equal pay, and balancing life and work.

Tracy Morgan plays Tracy Jordan, the unwieldy, unpredictable lead character of *TGS* whose hijinks and ludicrous behavior constantly get him into trouble (which Liz Lemon gets him out of). Tracy's character is often used to point out racial issues in society. He overcame an underprivileged background to become a high-paid movie and television star. While in many ways he seems to be playing a racial stereotype, he also has other qualities. He has been married to the same woman for over twenty years and loves his children dearly.

Other key figures of the show include writers or staff of *TGS*, who round out the quirky cast. Their onscreen antics reveal the real-life differences between performing and writing on a sketch comedy show and the conflicting interests they must somehow manage.

A Different Kind of Sitcom

Fey seamlessly brings together these vastly diverse personalities through her writing. *30 Rock* is a situation comedy (sitcom), although it diverges in some ways from traditional sitcoms. Storytelling is a much smaller part of the show's appeal than it is for other sitcoms. Many of Fey's jokes aren't dependent on the actual scene or the fact that it is about a sketch comedy show, making them universally funny. Instead, stand-alone moments and quick-witted lines form a much larger part of the show's backbone. These zingers come fast and frequently throughout each episode—so much so that it is easy for even the most attentive audience member to miss many of the jokes. (In fact, one blogger esti-mated that there were about ten jokes per minute in one 2010 episode.) The downside of such rapid delivery is that audience members may quickly get lost or lose interest, which may in part have contrib-uted to the show's less than stellar ratings.

Fey was new to sitcom writing, but she did develop a steady base of fans who helped keep the show running until its finale in 2013. Her talent also helped attract numerous notable faces to the show in hilarious cameos or guest spots. Many a celeb-rity—including some of the most recognizable faces in politics, Hollywood, and the world of music—graced the halls of Studio 6H (where *TGS* is filmed). This list includes, but is not limited to the likes of: Elizabeth Banks, Michael Bloomberg, Matt Damon, Robert De Niro, Al Gore, Jon Hamm, Tom Hanks, Salma Hayek, Paul McCartney, Condoleezza Rice, Martin Scorsese, and Oprah Winfrey, among many, many others.

TINA FEY'S COMEDY STYLES

Tina Fey uses many types of comedy in her writing. Here are a few of the genres or styles of comedy that Fey employed both in *30 Rock* and *SNL* and even some of her film roles.

character comedy: This method revolves around a persona created by an actor or comedian.

deadpan comedy: Comedians who employ this style tell jokes without changing facial expressions.

high comedy: This style of comedy relies on witty dialogue and biting humor and criticism of culture or society.

improvisational (improv) comedy: This style of comedy relies on actors' ability to create characters and plot with no (or very little) script.

low comedy: This style of comedy is often lewd and suggestive, many times employing physical humor.

parody/spoof: Parodies and spoofs recreate a book/film/play/television show or exaggerates the styles or mannerisms of particular individuals in a way that makes fun of them.

(continued on the next page)

(continued from the previous page)

prop comedy: This genre of comedy relies on props of a ridiculous nature or everyday objects used for comic effect.

satire: This form of comedy pokes fun at pop culture, current affairs, and news headlines through exaggeration, sarcasm, ridicule, and other tools.

sketch: This style of comedy involves short scripted pieces (such as those on *SNL* or *MadTV*). A sketch may involve the use of other forms of humor, such as satire, prop comedy, or others.

slapstick: In this style of comedy, exaggerated physical activity (such as pratfalls) are used for humorous effect.

surreal comedy: This style of comedy is based on bizarre or absurd situations and nonsense logic that defies common sense.

The Legacy of *30 Rock*

Although *30 Rock* lagged somewhat in popularity, it was critically acclaimed. Through the course of its seven seasons, *30 Rock* was nominated for 103 Emmys, including six consecutive nominations

for Outstanding Comedy Series (2007–13). In 2008
Alec Baldwin won the Emmy for Outstanding Lead
Actor in a Comedy Series and Tina Fey won for
Outstanding Lead Actress in a Comedy Series. The
2007 Golden Globes acknowledged *30 Rock* by
giving the series the award for Best Actor in Series—
Musical or Comedy (Alec Baldwin), and in 2008, it
won for Best Actress in Series—Musical or Comedy
(Tina Fey).

   The show went on to be nominated for numerous Emmy awards, Golden Globes, and more in
later years and secured a few more wins. *30 Rock*
was hailed as a twenty-first century *Mary Tyler
Moore Show*. Like the popular 1970s sitcom, *30
Rock* is about a woman who is a transplant to New
York City and tries her best to navigate the world
of media and her personal life, while still making audiences laugh. It also skillfully shines a light
onto some of the social problems facing the world.
Just like the sitcom from nearly forty years earlier,
30 Rock managed to provide its audience tears
and laughter, while still entertaining and producing
thought-provoking scenes.

CHAPTER
FIVE

Fey and Film

In addition to her numerous television credits, Fey has made her way onto the silver screen on several occasions. Her first major foray into the world of film was in 2004 when she wrote the screenplay for the cult classic *Mean Girls* and appeared as a teacher and mentor figure for the protagonist. She went on to appear in an assortment of other feature films, though none (as of yet) attained the popularity of *Mean Girls*, and she has yet to try her hand at another screenplay. Still, her charm on the screen is apparent, and many fans eagerly await her upcoming movie projects.

Mean Girls

In 2004, Tina Fey made her first major big-screen appearance in the film *Mean Girls*, which she also wrote. It was based on the nonfiction self-help book for parents of teenage girls *Queen Bees and Wannabes* by Rosalind Wiseman. The book

Tim Meadows and Tina Fey have fun on the set of *Mean Girls*. Another Second City and *SNL* alum, Meadows had worked with Fey before starring with her as the adults in charge at North Shore High School.

is meant to help parents advise their daughters how best to navigate the high school world of female cliques and deal with the aggressively mean behavior of many high school girls.

Because the book was written as a guidance book—and therefore had no plot—Fey had to create the plot from scratch. She was still serving as head writer at *SNL* at the time and had never written a screenplay. Even *30 Rock* was a few years away.

So she had to get creative. She was influenced by her own experiences at Upper Darby High School, when she saw firsthand the way girls would treat each other, run each other through the proverbial mud, and shame each other for their behavior. She did many rewrites and got Lorne Michaels to serve as producer on the film. Fey initially wanted the film to be a more raw depiction of high school, but when the studio asked her to make it PG-13, she moderated the tone—something she was used to doing when writing for *SNL*. As a sketch writer, she was also used to writing for other people more than herself—one of the reasons she has a relatively minor role in the film.

Fey has always openly talked about her feelings about the modern woman. She has said in interviews, in her book *Bossypants*, and, most obviously, in the film that girl-on-girl sabotage is one of the worst things women can do to one another. In a world dominated by men, women should be helping each other up, not pulling each other down.

Plot

Mean Girls centers around Cady (pronounced KAIT-EE) Heron (Lindsay Lohan), a sixteen-year old who has spent her life in Africa, studying wildlife with her zoologist parents. When her mother is offered a professorship with tenure, the family

QUEEN BEES AND WANNABES

A candid, poignant and sometimes painful look at the world of teenage girls, *Queen Bees and Wannabes* attempts to help parents advise daughters who might be dealing with the drama and trauma of high school. The book discuses the difficulties girls face: being teased mercilessly for the smallest things like wearing the wrong outfit or having interests outside of the social norm. Girls get branded with reputations that are often inaccurate and stick with them for their high school careers. Friends may give them bad advice, be bad influences, or outright hurt them. And teenage boys can be just as bad but are often clueless or oblivious to the feelings of girls. Many teenage girls feel their parents can't understand and have no idea what it is like to be a teenager.

All of these issues are highlighted in *Mean Girls*: from the outfits the protagonist Cady is made to wear when she's a part of the popular group, the "Plastics," to the "Burn Book" (in which nasty things are written about students and faculty at the school) to the romantic relationships between the various characters. Even Cady's relationship with her parents reflects many teens' belief that parents don't understand the issues facing them.

moves to Evanston, Illinois, where Cady attends school for the first time. Fictional North Shore High School is Cady's first introduction into "girl world."

New classmates Janis (Lizzy Caplan) and Damien (Daniel Franzese) befriend her and help her learn her way around high school. Through their guidance, Cady is introduced to the Plastics, a group of girls who seem perfect: wealthy, beautiful, and rulers of the school. Their queen bee is Regina George (Rachel McAdams), who, intrigued by Cady, invites her to join them at lunch. Janis sees an opportunity to infiltrate them, and asks Cady to play along so Janis can get revenge for the awful things Regina has said about her. Although she is academically inclined and feels more comfortable with the school's Mathletes than the Plastics, Cady agrees.

At Regina's house, Cady discovers all the ways girls can feel bad about their physical appearance: bad fingernail beds, big hips, huge calves, "man shoulders," hairlines, and pores. She also discovers the Burn Book: a mean, rumor-filled book that has terrible things written about all of her classmates and some of her teachers. She even adds to it, unwittingly, about Damien, and later, intentionally, about her teacher and mentor, Ms. Norbury (Tina Fey).

As she tries to find her place in the school, Cady becomes caught up in an awkward love triangle with none other than Regina's exboyfriend, Aaron Samuels (Jonathan Bennett). As her relationship with Regina sours, Cady also begins to turn Regina's

In an iconic scene from *Mean Girls*, Regina George (Rachel McAdams, center), asks Cady (Lindsay Lohan, standing) to join her and her friends for lunch. Amanda Seyfried (*left*) and Lacey Chabert (*right*) play the other Plastics.

Plastics—self-conscious Gretchen Weiners (Lacey Chabert) and dense Karen Smith (Amanda Seyfried) —against using Regina's own techniques: gossip, manipulation, and mean-spirited comments.

Essentially, Cady has made herself in Regina's image, unknowingly. The film then focuses on Cady's realization of this truth and her redemption— making peace with the people she hurt along the way and finding out how to be true to herself and her interests—with equal parts humor and sensitivity.

The Legacy of *Mean Girls*

Mean Girls was a minor hit, making about $129 million in box office revenue over its run. However, over the years since its release, *Mean Girls* has developed a cult following, as well as an ever-growing fan base. Not only has it inspired endless memes, GIFs, Facebook status updates, tweets, and Instagram posts, but it has continued to shine a light on the world of girl on girl "crime," in which cyber bullying, physical bullying, and other forms of social aggression sadly continue to be a part of many teens' daily lives.

The film has also influenced other realms of pop culture. Mariah Carey's 2009 hit "Obsessed" is inspired by the Regina George quote "Why are you so obsessed with me?" The audio is even used in the single. October 3 has been named *Mean Girls* day in honor of the scene in the movie in which Aaron asks Cady what day it is.

Even made-up words in the film have caught on in real life. "Fetch" actually did happen, but not in the way Gretchen ever wanted it to. "Grool," an awkward combination of "great" and "cool" invented by Cady when talking to Aaron, has also become a common phrase.

It is a film that adults, who have already lived

Tina Fey poses with Jonathan Bennett (*center*) and Lindsay Lohan (*right*) at the Los Angeles premiere of *Mean Girls* in April 2004. The film received great reviews and has since achieved status as one of the best teen comedies of all time.

through that sort of high school trauma, still find funny. And it appeals to teenagers and tweens alike. It seems ridiculous and obscene. But it is true in its reflection that this is what high school can be like. Fey tried her best to prepare girls for that. It's the message she'd been trying to spread for a long time to women and girls of all ages, from all walks of life: Life is funny. Life is hard. And there's no reason for anyone to make it any harder on anyone else than it has to be.

Other Films

After the success of *Mean Girls*, it seems that Fey became more comfortable on the big screen. In 2008, she made her next big film, *Baby Mama*, with fellow Second City and *SNL* alum and good friend Amy Poehler. In this movie, she plays a successful single woman looking for someone to be the surrogate mother of her child. She hires a dysfunctional woman (Poehler) who becomes pregnant. The film follows Fey'e character as she juggles preparing for motherhood with her romantic life and her developing friendship with her surrogate. Following *Baby Mama*, Fey voiced various characters in animated films and also made several other movies in which she got to work with both friends and influential actors.

In 2010, she made *Date Night* with Steve Carrell, in which the two play a married couple trying to have a date night that goes horribly and humorously wrong. In 2013, she starred in *Admission* with Paul Rudd, in which she plays an overworked college admissions officer who gets sidetracked by her attraction for a teacher who works with underprivileged children. In the same year she voiced a character on an episode of the animated television show *The Simpsons.*

In 2014, Tina strayed a bit from her slapstick sketch comedy roles and played Wendy Altman in the film *This is Where I Leave You*. The plot of the film revolves around four grown siblings who must live under the same roof together for a week, following their father's dying request. Although funny at times, the role represented a darker, more emotional one than anything Fey had ever done before. It was not widely seen, or highly reviewed, but reviewers did hail Fey for her work.

Other notable film appearances include Fey's work in the 2014 feature *Muppets Most Wanted*, a lighthearted family musical comedy in which Fey plays a Russian prison guard. While the Muppets are, naturally, the central focus of the film, the film boasts many entertaining cameos by high profile actors and entertainers. Fey's next major film role was as Katie Ellis in the 2015 comedy *Sisters*, in which she was reunited with her pal Amy Poehler. The pair play two sisters who throw a party in their parents' home before it is sold. She also stars in the 2016 film *Fun House*, opposite Martin Freeman in which she plays a war correspondent reporting in Afghanistan and Pakistan.

Although Fey cut her teeth in television, it is clear to anyone watching her that the multitalented actress is as at home on the big screen as she is on the small screen. No matter her medium, she always gives her fans something to look forward to.

CHAPTER
SIX

The Next Chapter for Tina Fey

In 2001, Tina Fey married her longtime boyfriend Jeff Richmond (who crafted the opening music for *30 Rock*). In 2005, as she was ending her tenure on *SNL* and ironing out the kinks in *30 Rock*, Tina gave birth to their first daughter, Alice Zenobia Richmond. On August 10, 2011, Fey and Richmond welcomed their second daughter, Penelope Athena Richmond.

Balancing Stardom and Motherhood

Motherhood changed Fey tremendously. While her humor never changed, she found herself even more passionate about women's issues, health, and child advocacy. She has been a spokeswoman for both the Mercy Corps (which is an organization that provides global relief in the

Tina Fey and husband Jeff Richmond have known each other for over twenty years. They married in 2001 and have two daughters together. Richmond is a musician and producer who often collaborates with his wife.

fight against world hunger), as well as Love Our Children USA (which works to end violence against children). She has also been active in supporting Autism Speaks, an organization that advocates for autism research and awareness. In 2015, she and her husband even auctioned off miscellaneous items from their home to raise money for the Leukemia & Lymphoma Society.

This is only one appearance of Fey's ability to balance being a mother and a writer/actress in the public eye. She referenced it in multiple episodes of *30 Rock*, as Liz struggles to adopt and then redefine the role as working mother in a way that works for her. Fey also took on film roles that reflect the lives and concerns of working mothers. *Baby Mama* (2008), for example, was about a hard-working single woman who employs a down-on-her luck woman to carry her baby. *Date Night* (2010) is about a husband and wife who are so consumed with jobs and parenting that they haven't had time for themselves.

Some of Fey's film roles after becoming a mother reflect a desire to make films that her daughters would enjoy watching. She was the voice of Roxanne Ritchie in *Megamind* in 2010 and starred in *Muppets Most Wanted* in 2014. She also made appearances on *Sesame Street* (2007) *SpongeBob SquarePants* (2009), and *iCarly* (2012). In 2011, she

Fey finds ways to balance motherhood and her career. Here, she is seen with daughter Alice on the set of *Baby Mama*, her film with friend and fellow comedian Amy Poehler (*left*).

narrated a radio special called *Hidden World of Girls*, which highlighted some spectacular women and girls telling their own stories. Fey shared some of her own memories of girlhood and her mother. In 2015, she narrated the nature documentary film *Monkey Kingdom*.

Comedian for all Ages

In 2011, Fey released her autobiography *Bossypants*—a hilarious, tongue-in-cheek, honest look into her life, from her childhood in Upper Darby to her time at Second City and *SNL*. Fey discusses motherhood, women's issues with beauty in the media (including her own body weight issues and her skepticism of interviews of both herself and other women in Hollywood who are asked for their beauty secrets), her relationship with her husband and with her famous *SNL* friends, and much, much more. Before its release, there had been rumors that the book had inspired a bidding war between many high-profile publishers. After its release, the book topped the *New York Times* "Best Sellers" list for five weeks. The audiobook was even nominated for a Grammy Award. It sold one million copies in its first year alone.

Fey also made headlines when she, along with Amy Poehler, cohosted the 70th Annual Golden Globe Awards in 2013. This was another variation of

Bossypants made Fey even more popular. Her dry wit and her ability to make almost any situation funny shone through on each page, just as it had for years on screen.

Fey's comedic genius: she dressed in ball gowns, did musical numbers, and shared the stage with some of the most esteemed and glamorous stars in Hollywood. And she did it flawlessly. So flawlessly, in fact that she was nominated for an Emmy and was asked to do it again with Poehler the next two years. She won her eighth Writers Guild of America Award for the 71st Golden Globe Awards.

As hosts, Fey and Poehler brought their satirical comedy to the stage of the prestigious awards show. The poked fun at the Hollywood elite in the audience: from the hours they spend getting camera ready, to their diets and fear of aging, to their attitudes, and in 2015, even called them "spoiled brats." They discussed the stereotypes of women in Hollywood (joking that there are no roles for women over forty unless you're Meryl Streep). Ultimately, they did what they do best: poke fun at the ridiculous situations of modern life and celebrity obsession. In 2015, they hosted the Golden Globes for the third and final time.

What's Next for Tina Fey?

In addition to Emmys, Golden Globes, Screen Actors Guild, and Writers Guild of America awards, Fey won the Mark Twain Prize for American Humor in 2010. At forty years old, she was the youngest to win this prestigious honor. Although Fey has earned

Tina Fey and Amy Poehler look glamorous as they poke fun at Hollywood's elite at the 72nd Annual Golden Globe awards. The pair hosted the show for the third and final time in 2015.

dozens of award nominations and awards over the course of her career; however, she's not done yet. She still has many projects up her sleeve.

On March 6, 2015, the first season of

THE MARK TWAIN PRIZE FOR AMERICAN HUMOR

Named for the famed American author and humorist Mark Twain, the Mark Twain Prize for American Humor is presented each year by the Kennedy Center in

On November 9, 2010, Tina Fey was awarded the Mark Twain Prize for American Humor. There was a special ceremony held at the Kennedy Center in Washington, D.C.

Washington, D.C., to an American entertainer who has had a positive impact on society. Like Mark Twain himself, the recipients of the prize have not been afraid to speak their minds—especially uncomfortable truths that others in society may not want to face.

The prize has been given to someone every year since 1998. Recipients of the award include Richard Pryor (1998), *SNL* creator and producer Lorne Michaels (2004), Steve Martin (2005), George Carlin (2008), Ellen DeGeneres (2012), and Eddie Murphy (2015). Fey was the 2010 recipient. Her friends, former *SNL* colleagues, and others turned out to honor Fey, who was only the third female to win the prize. Unlike previous winners, Fey was still at the top of her career, making her a unique choice. The combination of social commentary and humor that she has been able to communicate in her writing and performances have demonstrated her importance as both a comic and social observer.

Unbreakable Kimmy Schmidt was released on the popular movie streaming website Netflix. The thirteen-episode first season was originally slotted for NBC but was ultimately sold to Netflix. It was immediately picked up for a second season.

The show stars *30 Rock* alum Jane Krakowski (as an Upper West Side trophy wife) and Tituss Burgess (as an aspiring actor) in supporting roles for Ellie Kemper who plays the title role. Guest stars include Martin Short (playing a plastic surgeon), Jon Hamm (as the Reverend Richard Wayne Gary Wayne), Amy Sedaris (an Upper West Side woman struggling with her divorce), and of course, Tina Fey herself (as a completely incompetent lawyer). This female-driven comedy is in some ways similar to *30 Rock* and in other ways, quite different. The show was nominated for seven Primetime Emmy Awards in 2015 and won two.

The show revolves around a young woman who

The cast of *Unbreakable Kimmy Schmidt* discuss the show in Beverly Hills, California, in 2015. From left to right on stage are Tituss Burgess, Ellie Kemper, Tina Fey, creator/executive producer Robert Carlock, and Jane Krakowski.

was kidnapped at fifteen and forced to live under-
ground in a bunker, having been told by Reverend
Richard Wayne Gary Wayne that the world had
ended and outside the bunker there were lakes of
fire and monsters. Upon her rescue fifteen years
later, Kimmy moves to New York City in order to
experience the world. Naturally, she is naive and
gullible, but with the help of friends she meets and
her unbreakable spirit she manages to persevere.

So, what does Fey say she wants to do now?
More films and more television. She wants to
write and produce and direct more movies for
the big screen and has already been shopping
some screenplays around. In August 2015, it was
announced that Tina Fey had sold another pilot to
NBC. No details about the upcoming series are yet
known, but it is sure to be as addictive and hilarious
as her other projects.

Tina Fey has not only overcome the boys' world
that has been comedy writing for the last few
decades, but she has inspired many other comedians and the next generation of writers. Mindy
Kaling, Amy Schumer, and many more have all
hailed Fey as an inspiration and have expressed
a desire to work with her. (Amy Schumer got that
privilege in 2015 when Tina appeared in a sketch
on her show, *Inside Amy Schumer.*) Generations
of fans, male and female alike, eagerly wait to see

Fey poses on the red carpet of the Toronto International Film Festival. With many different feathers in her cap, it is clear Tina Fey can do anything she sets her mind to.

what the versatile and hilarious writer and comedian has in store next. Reviewers and fellow writers have called her "Goddess of the Geeks," "The Once and Future Queen," and even "the funniest woman in the world." Any and all of these are true. But the thing about Fey that fans must remember: she is a self-made woman who wants to promote equality among the sexes, the value of family, and being true to oneself. Fey herself admits that those qualities, along with her work ethic, are what have gotten her to where she is today. Her candid look at the world and her ability to blend the smart with the vulgar have made her humor a national treasure. But much more is sure to come. She will give us many more laughs, many more tears, and many more years of inspiration.

Fact Sheet ON TINA FEY

Name: Elizabeth Stamatina Fey
Parents: Zenobia "Jeanne" Fey and Don Fey
Siblings: Peter Fey (eight years older)
Birthdate: May 18, 1970
Birthplace: Upper Darby, Pennsylvania
Childhood Home: Upper Darby, Pennsylvania
Childhood Aspiration: To be on *Second City Televison*
Grade School(s) Attended: Cardington-Stonehurst Elementary, Beverly Hills Middle School
High School Attended: Upper Darby High School
College Attended: University of Virginia
Current Residence: New York, New York
Marital Status: Married to Jeff Richmond
Children: Two daughters: Alice Zenobia (born September 10, 2005), and Penelope Athena (born August 10, 2011)
First Stage Appearance: Upper Darby High School's Summer Stage
First Paid Stage Gig: Member of Second City tour group in 1994
First Television Appearance: As an extra on an episode of *Saturday Night Live* in 1999
First Regular Television Role: As coanchor of *Weekend Update* on *Saturday Night Live* in 2000
First Television Show Created: *30 Rock*
Current Job: Writer, actress, producer, creator, mother

Fact Sheet ON TINA FEY'S WORK

Writing Credits

1999–2006 *Saturday Night Live*, 130 episodes

2002 *The Colin Quinn Show*, 3 episodes; NBC 75th Anniversary Special

2004 *Mean Girls*

2006–13 *30 Rock*, 31 episodes

2013 70th Annual Golden Globes Awards

2014 71st Annual Golden Globe Awards

2015 72nd Annual Golden Globe Awards, *Saturday Night Live 40th Anniversary Special*, *Unbreakable Kimmy Schmidt*, 2 episodes

Television Credits

1999 *Upright Citizens Brigade*, Kerri Downey

1999–2006 *Saturday Night Live*, cast member

2006–13 *30 Rock*, Liz Lemon

2008–13 *Saturday Night Live,* host/guest star

2007 *Sesame Street*, one episode, Bookaneer Captain

2009 *SpongeBob SquarePants*, one episode, as herself

2011 *Phineas and Ferb*, one episode, Annabelle (voice)

2012 *iCarly,* one episode, as herself

2013 *Conan*, one episode, Conan; *The Simpsons*, Ms. Cantwell (voice); *The Awesomes*, The Advocate (voice)

2014–15 *Unbreakable Kimmy Schmidt*, 3 episodes, Marcia Clark

2015 *Inside Amy Schumer,* one episode, as herself

Film Credits

2002 *Martin & Orloff*, Southern Woman

2004 *Mean Girls*, Ms. Norbury

2006 *Beer League*, front desk girl; *Man of the Year*, herself

2007 *Aqua Teen Hunger Force Colon Movie Film for Theaters*, Burrito (voice)

2008 *Baby Mama*, Kate; *Ponyo*, Lisa (English version, voice)

2009 *The Invention of Lying*, Shelley

2010 *Date Night*, Claire Foster; *Megamind*, Roxanne Ritchie (voice)

2013 *Admission*, Portia Nathan; *Anchorman 2: The Legend Continues*, *Entertainment Tonight* reporter (uncredited)

2014 *Muppets Most Wanted,* Nadya; *This Is Where I Leave You*, Wendy Altman

2015 *Sisters*, Katie Ellis

2016 *Fun House*, Kim Barker

Books

Fey, Tina. *Bossypants*. New York, NY: Reagan Arthur/ Little Brown, 2011.

Quotes

Tina Fey on not being on Twitter, as told to Tituss Burgess: "Why would I give my jokes away for free?"

Critical Reviews

"Today's comediennes are on television, where they are often responsible for their own material. Tina Fey, for instance. The former head writer of *Saturday Night Live*, who wrote the film *Mean Girls* before creating the sitcom *30 Rock*, is one of the leading voices in a new generation of comediennes—women who not only play comic roles but also perform stand-up and write and direct comedy."
—Alessandra Stanley, *Vanity Fair,* April, 2008

"Fey, the star and creator of the NBC sitcom *30 Rock*, has been one of the strongest forces in comedy for the last 10 years. She gives voice to decent, hardworking people who are trying to make it through life without being pulled under by their own neuroses.... Fey is always great, even in American Express commercials."
—Jim Windolf, *Vanity Fair,* April, 2008

"NBC's parent company, General Electric, should send Senator John McCain flowers and a microwave oven. Tina Fey probably doesn't do a credible Mitt Romney, but her impersonation of Gov. Sarah Palin is so deliciously dead-on that it has helped 'Saturday Night Live' score its highest ratings in years."
—Alessandra Stanley, *New York Times*, October 29, 2008

"Journalists are constantly asking Tina Fey if she is totally surprised by her success. This is partly to do with the fact that she is the most unlikely glamour-puss ever to triumph on such a grand scale: a glasses geek turned writer turned TV star turned movie star turned presidential-election-year sensation turned household name."
—Jonathan Van Meter, *Vogue*, February 2010

"Her writing here isn't quite what you'd expect of a typical comedian's book—there are a number of joke-free paragraphs, and, like Liz Lemon, Fey the author isn't afraid to pontificate. She covers a lot of ground in a few short pages: the trials of being an extraordinarily busy working mom; women over 40 in Hollywood; having children later in life."
—Stephen Lee, *Entertainment Weekly*, February 11, 2011

"She's gotten even more famous because of her bestselling memoir, *Bossypants*. It lit a fire under the already raging Tina Fey cult, no doubt in part because it came out when Oprah was going off the air and we needed a new American superhero queen."
—Rob Sheffield, *Rolling Stone*, February 17, 2012

"Something about this movie-star mockery, in our time of ongoing social and cultural anguish— police brutality, Charlie Hebdo—felt deeply right. It was delicious. Or maybe it was just that giddy feeling of being affectionately teased by someone you love."
—Sarah Larson, *New Yorker*, January 15, 2015

"Not only am I excited to see the women Fey might create next, but I'm also interested to watch who she mentors and where they go."
—Alyssa Rosenburg, slate.com, September 25, 2015

Timeline

1970 Elizabeth Stamatina Fey is born in Upper Darby, Pennsylvania.

1988 Tina Fey graduates from Upper Darby High School.

1992 Fey graduates from the University of Virginia with a bachelor's degree in drama.

1992 Fey moves to Chicago.

1994 Fey begins at famed improv theater Second City and starts dating future husband Jeff Richmond.

1997 Fey begins writing for *Saturday Night Live*.

1999 Fey becomes head writer of *Saturday Night Live*. *Dratch & Fey* premiers at Second City in Chicago and at Upright Citizens Brigade in New York City

2000 Fey begins coanchoring "Weekend Update" on *Saturday Night Live*.

2001 *Entertainment Weekly* names Fey one of the entertainers of the year. Fey marries Jeff Richmond.

2004 Fey writes and stars in *Mean Girls*.

2005 Fey wins a Writer's Guild of America Award for Best Adapted Screenplay. Fey's first daughter with Richmond, Alice Zenobia Richmond, is born

2006 Fey retires from *Saturday Night Live*. *30 Rock* premieres.

2007 Fey participates in the Writer's Guild strike. Fey appears on *Time* magazine's annual "100" list of the most influential people of that year.

2008 Fey stars in *Baby Mama* with Amy Poehler. Fey voices Lisa in the English version of the Japanese film *Ponyo*. Fey debuts her impersonation of Governor Sarah Palin on *Saturday Night Live*, bumping up her celebrity status and the viewership of both *SNL* and *30 Rock*.

2009 Fey plays Shelley in *The Invention of Lying*. Fey again appears on the *Time* "100" list. Fey buys an apartment on the Upper West Side of Manhattan with her husband.

2010 Fey stars opposite Steve Carrell in *Date Night* as Claire Foster. Fey voices Roxanne Ritchie in *Megamind*. Fey wins the Mark Twain Prize for American Humor.

2011 Fey gets a star on the Hollywood Walk of Fame. Fey's second daughter with Richmond, Penelope Athena, is born. *Bossypants* is published. Fey narrates the radio documentary *Hidden World of Girls*.

2013 Fey plays Portia Nathan in *Admission* with Paul Rudd. Fey appears as an *Entertainment Tonight* reporter in *Anchorman 2: The Legend Continues*. *30 Rock* airs its final episode. Fey cohosts The 70th Golden Globe Awards with Amy Poehler.

2014 Fey produces and stars as Nadya in *Muppets Most Wanted*. Fey stars as Wendy Altman in *This Is Where I Leave You*. Fey hosts the 71st Golden Globe Awards with Amy Poehler.

2015 *Unbreakable Kimmy Schmidt* premieres on Netflix. Fey narrates a nature documentary, *Monkey Kingdom*. Fey hosts the 72nd Golden Globe Awards with Amy Poehler. Fey appears on *Inside Amy Schumer* as herself. Fey stars as Katie Ellis alongside Amy Poehler in *Sisters*. Fey sells a new untitled pilot to NBC.

2016 Fey stars as Kim Baker in *Fun House*.

Glossary

cameo An appearance on a television show, play, or film made by a well-known celebrity that is usually one time only.

character comedy The use by an actor of a persona he or she has created in a scene or sketch.

deadpan Maintaining a neutral facial expression while telling a joke.

guest star Someone who appears in a television show, play, or film for a period of time or in a recurring role.

high comedy Comedy that requires previous knowledge in order to appreciate it; usually includes satire and/or parody.

improv A style of comedy that is done without a script in which the actors must create a scene in the moment.

inaugural Characterizing the first or beginning of something.

low comedy Comedy that is simple in its execution: usually physical and rather vulgar and appealing to base instincts

mock To make fun of something.

parody A scene, play, film, or television show that makes fun of and works with the style of a piece that is already well known.

poignant Strong in feeling or emotion; appealing to the mind.

producer Someone who manages a television show

or film and is usually in charge of budgets, hiring/firing, as well as many other day-to-day tasks in running the production.

prop comedy The use of props or outlandish costumes in order to advance a scene or action.

satire The use of many forms of comedy (including irony, deadpan, and slapstick) to poke fun at society, including pop culture, politics, and individuals.

sitcom Short for situation comedy. A regularly broadcast television show with a group of characters who are often in humorous situations.

sketch A quick scene that is self-contained and usually humorous.

slapstick A style of comedy that is over-the-top, ostentatious, and boisterous. Examples include pratfalls and pies in actors' faces.

tongue-in-cheek A figure of speech used to mean that a statement, book, film, or other production is not meant to be taken completely seriously.

wit Keen perception that expresses clever ideas or thoughts.

For More Information

Canadian Improv Games
135 Séraphin-Marion
Ottawa, ON K1N 6N5
Canada
(613) 726-6339
Website: http://improv.ca/about/contact-us/#sthash.
    mbKcZNSg.dpuf
Since 1977, the Canadian Improv Games have
    gathered high school students all over Canada
    to explore improvisation in a supportive setting.
    The organization offers training in addition to
    organizing competitions.

The Comedy Cures Foundation
122 E. Clinton Avenue
Tenafly, NJ 07670
(201) 227-8410
Website: http://www.comedycures.org
Founded by cancer survivor Saranne Rothberg, The
    Comedy Cures Foundation brings comedy,
    through both entertainment and education, to
    children and adults suffering from illness,
    depression, disabilities, and other traumas.

The Groundlings
7307 Melrose Avenue
Los Angeles, CA 90046
(323) 934-4747
Website: http://www.groundlings.com

Delighting Los Angeles audiences for more than thirty-six years, this nonprofit organization stages performances and offers improv training for aspiring comedians. It has launched many successful stars including Kristin Wiig, Maya Rudolph, and Jimmy Fallon.

Kids 'N Comedy
173 W. 78th Street, #5A
New York, NY 10024
(212) 877-6115
Website: http://www.kidsncomedy.com
Writers and comedians make up the staff of Kids 'N Comedy. They teach teens and young adults about comedy through classes, workshops, and other programs.

The Second City Chicago
1616 N. Wells St.
Chicago, IL 60614
(312) 337-3992
Website: http://www.secondcity.com
For more than fifty years, the Second City has produced improv comedy theater in addition to offering classes and helping up-and-coming comedians find their voice.

The Second City Toronto
51 Mercer Street
Toronto, ON M5V 9G9
Canada

(416) 343-0011

Website: http://www.secondcity.com/shows/toronto/

An offshoot of the original Chicago location, the
Second City in Toronto produces improv shows
and offers classes for both children and adults.

Upright Citizens Brigade (UCB)

153 E. 3rd Street

New York, NY 10009

(212) 366-9176

website: http://www.ucbtheatre.com

Like Second City, UCB offers classes as well as
shows for the aspiring sketch comedian. It now
has two locations in New York City and two in
Los Angeles.

Websites

Because of the changing nature of Internet links,
Rosen Publishing has developed an online list of
websites related to the subject of this book. This site
is updated regularly. Please use this link to access
the list:

http://www.rosenlinks.com/COMEDY/Fey

For Further Reading

Bent, Mike. *The Everything Guide to Sketch Comedy*. Avon, MA: Adams Media, 2009.

Castle, Alison. *Saturday Night: The Book*. New York, NY: Taschen, 2015.

Dratch, Rachel. *Girl Walks Into a Bar…Comedy Calamities, Dating Disasters, and a Midlife Miracle*. New York, NY: Gotham, 2012.

Fallon, Jimmy. *Thank You Notes*. New York, NY: Grand Central Publishing, 2011.

Fey, Tina. *Bossypants*. New York, NY: Little, Brown, 2011.

Irwin, William, and J. Jeremy Wisnewski. *30 Rock and Philosophy: We Want to Go to There*. Hooken, NJ: Wiley Publishing. 2010.

Kaling, Mindy. *Is Everyone Hanging Out Without Me? (And Other Concerns)*. New York, NY: Three Rivers Press, 2012.

Kaling, Mindy. *Why Not Me?* New York, NY: Crown, 2015.

Kaplan, Steve. *The Hidden Tools of Comedy*. Burbank, CA: Michael Weise Productions, 2013.

Leonard, Kelly, and Tom Yorton. *Yes, And: How Improvisation Reverses "No, But" Thinking and Improves Creativity and Collaboration — Lessons from The Second City*. New York, NY: Comedy Council of Nicea, 2015.

Libera, Ann. *The Second City Almanac of Improvisation*. Chicago, IL: Northwestern University Press, 2004.

Miller, James Andrew, and Tom Shales. *Live From New York: The Complete, Uncensored History of Saturday Night Live as Told by Its Stars, Writers, and Guests*. Boston, MA: Little Brown and Company, 2014.

Perret, Gene. *Comedy Writing Self-Taught: The Professional Skill-Building Course in Writing Stand-Up, Sketch, and Situation Comedy*. Fresno, CA: Quill Driver Books, 2015.

Poehler, Amy. *Yes, Please*. New York, NY: Dey Street Books, 2015.

Thomas, Mike, *The Second City Unscripted: Revolution and Revelation at the World-Famous Comedy Theater*. Chicago, Illinois: Northwestern University Press, 2012.

Tropiano, Steve, *Saturday Nigh Live FAQ*. Montreal, QC, Canada: Applause Theatre and Cinema Books, 2013.

Walsh, Matt, Ian Roberts, and Matt Besser. *Upright Citizens Brigade Comedy Improvisational Manual*. New York, NY: Comedy Council of Nicea, 2013.

Bibliography

Bianculli, Dave. "Tina Fey: Sarah Palin And *Saturday Night Live.*" *Fresh Air*, NPR, November 3, 2008. Retrieved August 30, 2015 (http://www.npr.org/2013/01/25/170247016/tina-fey-sarah-palin-and-saturday-night-satire).

Dockterman, Eliana. "Why We Need More Women Creating TV Shows." *Time*, September 15, 2015. Retrieved September 20, 2015 (http://time.com/4034566/emmys-tina-fey-tv-shows/).

Dowd, Maureen. "What Tina Fey Wants." *Vanity Fair*, January 2009. Retrieved August 28, 2015 (http://www.vanityfair.com/culture/2009/01/tina_fey200901).

Fey, Tina. *Bossypants*. New York, NY: Little, Brown, 2011.

Fey, Tina. "Confessions of a Juggler." *New Yorker*, February 14, 2011. Retrieved September 20, 2015 (http://www.newyorker.com/magazine/2011/02/14/confessions-of-a-juggler).

Fey, Tina. "Lessons from Late Night." *New Yorker*, March 14, 2011. Retrieved September 20, 2015 (http://www.newyorker.com/magazine/2011/03/14/lessons-from-late-night).

Larson, Sarah. "Tina and Amy's Last Golden Globes." *New Yorker*, January 12, 2015. Retrieved September 19, 2015 (http://www.newyorker.com/culture/sarah-larson/tina-amys-last

-golden-globes).

Nepales, Ruben V. "Amy Poehler on Tina Fey: She Is My Chosen Sister." *Philippine Daily Inquirer*, June 19, 2015. Retrieved September 5, 2015 (http://entertainment.inquirer.net/172666 /amy-poehler-on-costar-tina-fey-she-is -my-chosen-sister).

Schneider, Michael. "Tina Fey" *Variety*, November, 8, 2009. Retireved September 3, 2015 (http:// variety.com/2008/scene/markets-festivals /tina-fey-3-1117996147/).

Stanley, Allessandra. "Who Says Women Aren't Funny?" *Vanity Fair*, April, 2008. Retrieved September 7, 2015 (http://www.vanityfair.com /news/2008/04/funnygirls200804).

Stein, Joel. "Goddess of the Geeks." *Time*, April 18, 2004. Retrieved August 15, 2015 (http:// content.time.com/time/magazine /article/0,9171,993922,00.html).

Steinberg, Jaques. "*30 Rock* Lives, and Tina Fey Laughs." *New York Times*, September 23, 2007. Retrieved September 5, 2015 (http:// www.nytimes.com/2007/09/23/arts /television/23stei.html).

Van Meter, Jonathan. "Tina Fey: Miss Tina Regrets." Vogue, February 15, 2015. Retrieved August 31, 2015 (http://www.vogue.com/865492 /miss-tina-regrets/).

Index

A

Admission, 76

B

Baby Mama, 39, 76, 80
Baldwin, Alec, 59, 61
Bossypants, 12, 15, 20, 22,
     25, 38, 46, 70, 82

C

Clinton, Hillary, 53, 55
comedians
     early jobs of famous
          comedians, 28–30

D

Date Night, 76, 80
Dratch, Rachel, 41–42, 45,
     48, 57, 59

F

Fey, Don, 10, 12, 15–16
Fey, Tina
     childhood, 7–8, 10–23
     children and motherhood,
          58, 78, 80–82
     comedy styles, 65–66
     education, 18–23, 24–27
     favorite childhood tv
          shows, 13–15
     marriage, 38–39, 41, 78
     philanthropy, 78–80
     scar, 16–18

G

Golden Globes, 36, 41, 67,
     82–84

I

improv
     rules of improv, 33–34, 37
ImprovOlympic Theater, 39

K

Krakowski, Jane, 56, 61–63,
     87

L

Lemon, Liz, 26, 61–63, 80

M

Mark Twain Prize, 84–87
Mary Tyler Moore Show,
     The, 13–14, 67
Mean Girls, 7, 19, 20
     book origins, 68–70, 71
     plot, 70–74
     popularity of, 74–75, 76
Michaels, Lorne, 43–44, 45,
     46, 48, 50, 59
Morgan, Tracy, 56, 63
Muppets Most Wanted, 77,
     80

N

"Nonpartisan Message from
     Governor Sarah Palin

and Senator Hillary
Clinton, A" 53

P

Palin, Sarah, 7, 49–50,
52–55
Pennsylvania
famous performers from,
20–21
Poehler, Amy, 8, 32, 36, 37,
38, 39–41, 45, 48, 49,
53, 76, 77, 82–84
as coanchor of "Weekend
Update," 51–52

Q

Queen Bees and
Wannabes, 68–69, 71

R

Richmond, Jeff, 38–39, 41,
78

S

Saturday Night Live, 7, 8,
13, 15, 25, 26, 33, 34,
42, 43, 59, 70, 76, 78, 82
Fey as first female head
writer, 44–48
Fey's most popular
sketches, 48–50
Fey's Sarah Palin impres-
sion, 52–55

Fey's time as "Weekend
Update" coanchor, 48,
50–52
influence on 30 Rock, 56,
57
SCTV, 32–33
Second City, 30–42, 43, 76,
82
famous alumni of, 34–36
Fey's time touring with,
37–38
Sisters, 39

T

30 Rock, 7, 26, 41, 46, 49,
52, 55, 56–57, 78, 80
critical reception, 66–67
guest stars, 64
how it differed from other
sitcoms, 63–64
origins of, 57–58
production of, 58–63
This Is Where I Leave You, 77

U

Unbreakable Kimmy
Schmidt, 87–89
University of Virginia, 24–27
Upper Darby High School,
18–20, 22–23, 24, 70
Upper Darby Summer
Stage, 22–23
Upright Citizen's Brigade, 41

About the Author

Kathryn Harrison has always had an interest in the world of entertainment. She began playing music at the age of four, and by the time she was a teenager, she was a regular player at the Ryman Auditorium in her hometown of Nashville, Tennessee. She attended the American Academy of Dramatic Arts in New York City and took many theater and improv classes at the Stella Adler Studio and Uta Hagen's HB Studio, as well as with the Upright Citizens Brigade. Pursuing her other great love, Kathryn began writing professionally as a young adult, and, much like Liz Lemon, enjoys singing along to musicals while she writes. She currently resides in New York City with her husband.

Photo Credits

Cover, p. 3 Helga Esteb/Shutterstock.com; cover background, interior pages (curtain) Kostsov/Shutterstock.com; pp. 6, 40-41, 54-55, 85 Theo Wargo/Getty Images; p. 12 Debra L Rothenberg/FilmMagic/Getty Images; pp. 14-15 NBC Television/Archive Photos/Getty Images; pp. 16-17 Dave Hogan/Hulton Archive/Getty Images; p. 25 Cindy Ord/Getty Images; p. 27 Joe Schilling/The LIFE Images Collection/Getty Images; pp. 28-29 Imeh Akpanudosen/Getty Images; pp. 36-37 KMazur/WireImage/Getty Images; p. 44 Kevin Mazur/WireImage/Getty Images; pp. 46-47 Jamie McCarthy/Getty Images; pp. 50-51 Jon Kopaloff/FilmMagic/Getty Images; pp. 58-59 Raleigh News & Observer/Tribune News Service/Getty Images; pp. 60-61 Jason Kempin/NBCUniversal/Getty Images; p. 66 Steve Mack/FilmMagic/Getty Images; pp. 68-69 Gilbert Carrasquillo/Getty Images; p. 75 Bloomberg/Getty Images; pp. 78-79 NBC/Photofest © NBC; p. 83 Kevin Winter/Getty Images.

Designer: Nicole Russo; Editor: Shalini Saxena; Photo Research: Bruce Donnola